Pathway to Grammar

Student's Book

Noelle Child

1

Richmond

Richmond
58 St Aldates
Oxford
OX1 1ST
United Kingdom

Pathway to Grammar Student's Book Level 1

First Edition: 2015
Sixth Reprint: February 2020
ISBN: 978-607-06-1081-3

Av. Río Mixcoac No. 274, Col. Acacias,
Benito Juárez, C.P. 03240, Ciudad de México

Publisher: Justine Piekarowicz
Editorial Team: Jennifer S. Li, Joep van der Werff
Art and Design Coordinator: Marisela Pérez
Design: Erika Martínez
Layout: Paola Romero
Pre-Press Coordinator: Daniel Santillán
Pre-Press Team: Susana Alcántara, Virginia Arroyo
Cover Design: Erika Martínez

Cover Photograph: ©**THINKSTOCK:** iStock (kwasny221, w_stockphoto); Photodisc (Digital Vision); Polka Dot (Jupiterimages)

Illustrations: Maya García pp. 16, 23, 35, 38, 56, 75; Gilberto Guzmán pp. 15, 37, 58, 59, 79; Alberto Morales pp. 7, 30, 45, 47; Alma Nuñez pp. 8, 11, 27, 28, 49, 66, 68; Tania Recio pp. 18, 40, 57; Ismael Vázquez pp. 17, 19, 20, 36, 39, 55, 61, 76, 78; Carlos Vélez pp. 6, 9, 26, 46, 51, 67, 70; David Yañez pp. 5, 10, 25, 29, 48, 53, 65, 69, 71

Photographs: ©**REPOSITORIO:** Ediciones Santillana, S.A. (Argentina) pp. 27, 33, 44; Editora Moderna, Ltda. p. 57; Editorial Santillana, S.A. (Guatemala) pp. 6, 13, 21, 43, 50; Richmond Publishing S.A. de C.V. p. 47 (Elias Hermann Salas Martínez); Santillana de Ediciones, S.A. p. 63; Santillana Educación S.L. pp. 33 (Amador Toril Díaz, TRECE POR DIECIOCHO IP digital estudio 2), 57 (HighRes Press Stock), 69 (Javier Jaime Sánchez); ©**THINKSTOCK:** amana images p. 59 (DAJ); BananaStock pp. 57 (BananaStock), 64 (BananaStock), 87 (BananaStock); Blend Images p. 64 (Jose Luis Pelaez Inc); Creatas p. 45 (Creatas); Design Pics p. 54 (Design Pics/Kristy-Anne Glubish); Digital Vision pp. 20 (Thomas Northcut), 25 (James Woodson), 41 (Christopher Robbins), 58 (Thomas Northcut, Digital Vision), 63 (Ryan McVay), 66 (Hoby Finn); Dorling Kindersley RF pp. 24 (Andy Crawford, Dave King), 28 (Dorling Kindersley), 57 (Dave King), 81 (Andy Crawford); Fuse pp. 35 (Susanne Dittrich/Fuse), 42 (Fuse), 54 (Fuse), 57 (Fuse), 59 (Fuse), 75 (Fuse), 81 (Fuse); Hemera pp. 4 (Alexey Romanov), 6 (Zeljko Bozic), 19 (Le Do, Uriy Badaev), 33 (Daniel Cole), 39 (Derek Audette), 41 (Ron Chapple studios, Sonya Etchison, Mikhail Dudarev), 42 (Andrei Kiselev), 54 (Piotr Marcinski), 62 (Jose manuel Gelpi diaz), 63 (Lucia Guiducci); Hemera Technologies p. 9 (PhotoObjects.net); IndiaPicture p. 59 (Amit Somvanshi); Ingram Publishing p. 63 (Ingram Publishing); iStock pp. 3-83 (Vladislav Ociacia), 4 (Christophe Testi, Catherine dée Auvil, kevin mayer, Brian Guest, Mariusz Blach, studiocasper, w_stockphoto, _human, GlobalP, abadonian), 5 (Christophe Testi, kevin mayer, Mariusz Blach, studiocasper, jojje9999, Szepy), 6 (Mariusz Blach, studiocasper, Eric Isselée, SergiyN, Issaurinko), 14 (Sociologas, Nastco, Eric Isselée, Jag_cz, PeJo29, rickmartinez, AlexMax, andrewburgess, simonkr, Périg MORISSE), 17 (Kenishirotie, LiuSol, Peter de Kievith, Dontwannastop, Donyanedomam, FrancescoRizzato, Chris Johnson), 19 (tiler84, Mile Atanasov, fotostok_pdv, joseyrosa, efesantik, Silense), 20 (w_stockphoto, fotostok_pdv, g-stockstudio, molishka1988, GlobalP, sunstock), 23 (michaeljung, 3sbworld, MrPants), 24 (Alex Kotlov, Murat Öz, alptraum, Iwona Grodzka, Milos Eric, Eric Isselée, koosen, Jani Bryson, aguirre_mar, sserg_dibrova, Jani Bryson, wathanyu, Valengilda), 25 (TatyanaGl, SergiyN), 26 (Coffeemill, tiler84, Taylor Hinton, 3sbworld, Silense, vencavolrab), 27 (koosen, SychuginaElena, witoldkr1, horillaz, AvalancheZ, bbtomas), 28 (EcoPic, Paffy69, Anton_Sokolov, SafakOguz, Sablin, kotomiti), 32 (Jose Manuel Gelpi Diaz, GlobalP, andriikoval, pjrimages, cynoclub), 33 (bbtomas, Iwona Grodzka), 34 (reanas, Nicole S. Young, ariwasabi, Kamil Macniak, Jacek Chabraszewski, de santis paolo, Eric Isselée, popovaphoto, karammiri, Issaurinko, MichaelJay, rgbdigital), 35 (gpointstudio, christingasner, StratosGiannikos), 37 (Tohid Hashemkhani, Tatiana Nizovteva, Evgeny Karandaev, Muralinath, design56, VladyslavDanilin, Buriy, ewastudio), 39 (mark wragg, Psonia, GooDween123, abadonian), 41 (dziewul, Melpomenem, PABimages), 42 (CREATISTA), 44 (monkeybusinessimages, NatalyaAksenova, lanych, Jeff Huting, MG, TuTheLens, ikachan999, mamahoohooba, pressureUA, Matthew Jones, amwu, GoodMood Photo), 45 (Anton Snarikov, irina88w, Dmitriy Shironosov, JZhuk, bernie_moto), 46 (Victoire_Lefevre), 47 (Sinelyov, LyndaPitts, cynoclub), 50 (colematt), 51 (Deyan Georgiev, SergiyN), 52 (Marzanna Syncerz), 53 (AndreyPopov), 54 (Wojciech Gajda, Jonathan Hill, Vlad Turchenko, 3sbworld, fotostok_pdv), 55 (TatyanaGl, monkeybusinessimages, Jani Bryson), 57 (vencavolrab, Okea, robertsrob, DutchScenery, Fesus Robert), 58 (Bernad Gavril, PaulineCheeseman, ziggy_mars, JStaley401), 59 (mrovka), 60 (Catherine Yeulet, irina88w), 62 (shironosov), 63 (3sbworld, ferlistockphoto, stokkete, ferlistockphoto, Ljupco, RossellaApostoli), 64 (arquiplay77, gkuna, Vitali Dyatchenko, Jani Bryson, SerrNovik, Jani Bryson, Ljupco, DrPAS, L_POP, Antonio Gravante, poligonchik, cynoclub), 66 (Viktor Čáp, Tammy Abrego, fotokostic, ajkkafe, michaeljung, nyul), 68 (Pavel Lipsky, M_a_y_a, Jani Bryson, castillodominici, neuson11, Yobro10, g-stockstudio), 69 (Catherine dée Auvil, Danny Hooks, Teerapun, RyanKing999, elcabron, vladimirkim3722), 72 (Ljupco, Nanette_Grebe, kaktyc, Roman_Gorielov), 74 (WestLight, Hyrma, Kenishirotie, KCHANDE, somchaij, Jiradelta, MikeyGen73, anna1311, pilipphoto, aarrows), 75 (Jani Bryson, 3sbworld, Silense, cynoclub, Lilun_Li), 76 (Ljupco, paulburns1, Kirill Zdorov, Jani Bryson, rosliothman, nickjamesstock, AndreyPopov, SlobodanMiljevic), 77 (AnjelaGr, DavidFR, anandaBGD, ffolas), 80 (yganko), 81 (futureimage, Andresr, McIninch, Ina Peters, monticelllo, Ornitolog82, popovaphoto, McIninch), 82 (KCHANDE, MikeyGen73, karelnoppe, monkeybusinessimages, Serhiy Shullye, Александр Перепелица), 83 (Serhiy Shullye, Natikka, multik7, Hyrma), 84 (Yobro10), 85 (vencavolrab, Fesus Robert, Andreas Rodriguez), 86 (Feng Yu, Devonyu, jeep5d), 88 (belchonock), 89 (Robert Churchill), 90 (photomaru, monticelllo), 91 (loops7, anna1311); Lite Productions p. 45 (Lite Productions); Monkey Business pp. 41 (Monkey Business Images), 72 (Monkey Business Images), 74 (Monkey Business Images Ltd); moodboard p. 54 (moodboard); Photodisc pp. 4 (Ryan McVay), 5 (Ryan McVay), 9 (Ryan McVay), 12 (Digital Vision), 22 (Flying Colours Ltd), 25 (Thomas Northcut), 34 (Ryan McVay), 35 (Digital Vision), 45 (Ryan McVay), 54 (Thomas Northcut), 55 (Photodisc), 64 (Photodisc), 66 (Digital Vision), 72 (Todd Warnock, Photodisc), 73 (Photodisc), 77 (Jack Hollingsworth), 81 (Barbara Penoyar); PhotoObjects.net pp. 4 (Photos.com), 5 (Photos.com), 39 (Photos.com), 41 (Hemera Technologies), 55 (Hemera Technologies), 80 (Hemera Technologies), 83 (Hemera Technologies); Photos.com pp. 4 (Jupiterimages), 5 (Jupiterimages); Polka Dot pp. 32 (Jupiterimages), 35 (Jupiterimages); Purestock pp. 17 (Purestock), 41 (Purestock); Stockbyte. pp. 4 (Brand X Pictures), 22 (altrendo images), 44 (Stockbyte), 54 (Comstock Images), 59 (Stockbyte), 64 (Jupiterimages), 76 (Stockbyte), 82 (Stockbyte), 83 (Stockbyte), 86 (George Doyle & Ciaran Griffin); Valueline p. 54 (Valueline); Wavebreak Media pp. 4 (Wavebreakmedia Ltd), 5 (Wavebreakmedia Ltd), 6 (Wavebreakmedia Ltd), 9 (Wavebreakmedia Ltd), 25 (Wavebreakmedia Ltd), 60 (Wavebreakmedia Ltd), 64 (Wavebreakmedia Ltd), 83 (Wavebreakmedia Ltd); Zoonar pp. 4 (Zoonar/N.Sorokin), 9 (Zoonar RF, Zoonar/E.Lam), 20 (Zoonar/unknown), 64 (Zoonar/O.Kovach), 76 (Zoonar RF)

Impressão e acabamento: Log&Print Gráfica e Logística S.A.
Lote: 748267
Printed in Brazil

Contents

Unit 1

alien

apple

book

cat

desk

elephant

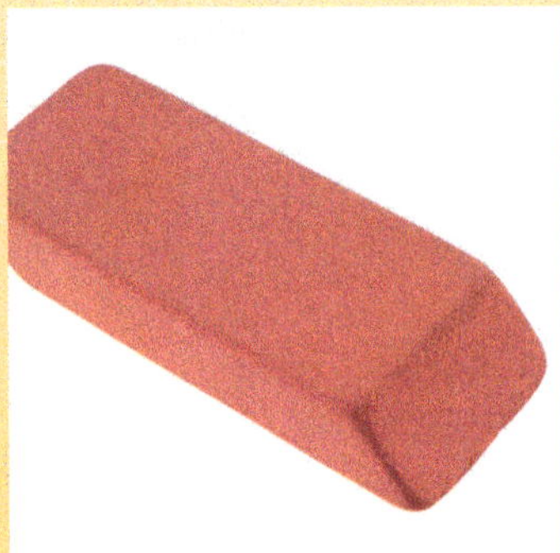

eraser

lunch box

orange (*n*)

pen

pencil

pictures

playground

ruler

school

teacher

a, an 1

A school? An elephant?

No. A playground!

1 Circle *a* or *an*, and match.

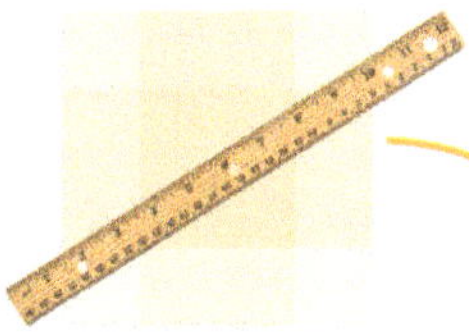

1. ***a*** / ***an*** ruler
2. ***a*** / ***an*** desk
3. ***a*** / ***an*** book
4. ***a*** / ***an*** orange
5. ***a*** / ***an*** teacher
6. ***a*** / ***an*** apple
7. ***a*** / ***an*** pencil
8. ***a*** / ***an*** eraser

1 Find, circle, and complete.

p	c	k	e	x	a	p	p	l	e
r	a	c	b	o	o	k	e	s	v
w	t	o	a	e	a	l	n	k	p
d	n	u	k	b	s	s	j	v	h
c	s	o	o	r	u	l	e	r	x
d	o	z	a	e	a	p	b	r	g
b	v	m	d	o	r	a	n	g	e
e	p	s	c	h	o	o	l	l	i
e	r	a	s	e	r	d	r	z	x

1.  *It's* *an* orange.
2.  *It's* *a* cat.
3.  *It's* _____ book.
4.  _____ _____ eraser.
5.  _____ _____ apple.
6.  _____ _____ pen.
7.  _____ _____ school.
8. 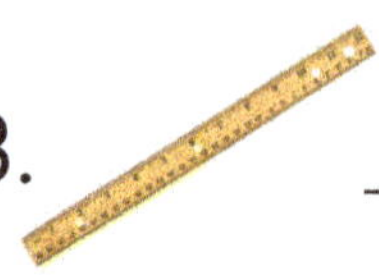 _____ _____ ruler.

It is not / It isn't

1 Look, mark (X), and color.

1

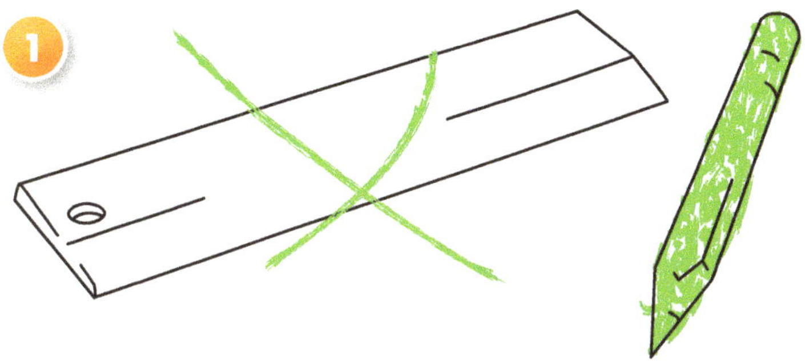

It isn't a ruler. It's a pencil.

2

It isn't an eraser. It's a teacher.

3

It isn't a school. It's a playground.

4

It isn't a cat. It's an elephant.

5

It isn't an apple. It's an orange.

6

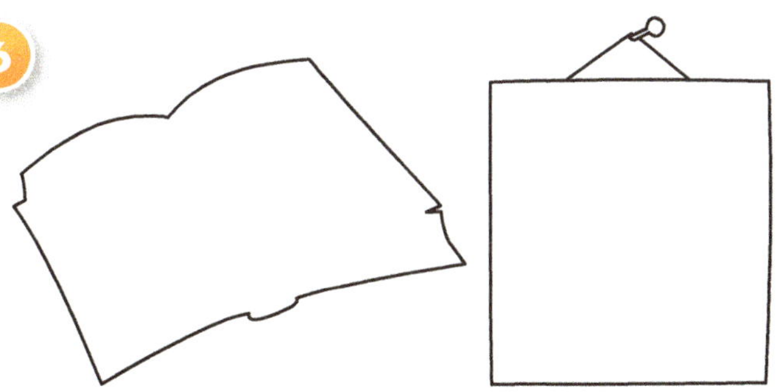

It isn't a picture. It's a book.

1 Look, follow, and write.

1. Is he a teacher?
   Yes, he is.
2. Is it a book?
   No, it isn't.
3. Is it an elephant?
   ______, ______ ______.
4. ______ ______ ______ apple?
   ______, ______ ______.
5. ______ ______ ______ lunch box?
   ______, ______ ______.
6. ______ ______ ______ cat?
   ______, ______ ______.

They are / They're

1 Look and write.

1 

They're books.

2 

__________ erasers.

3 

__________ __________.

4 

__________ __________.

2 Complete and draw.

They're __________.

1 Read, color, and write.

1. They're desks.

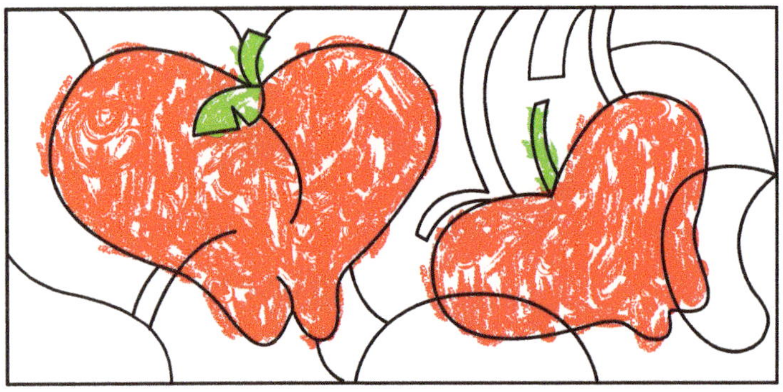

They aren't desks.

They're apples.

2. They're erasers.

__________ __________ erasers.

____________________ pens.

3. They're elephants.

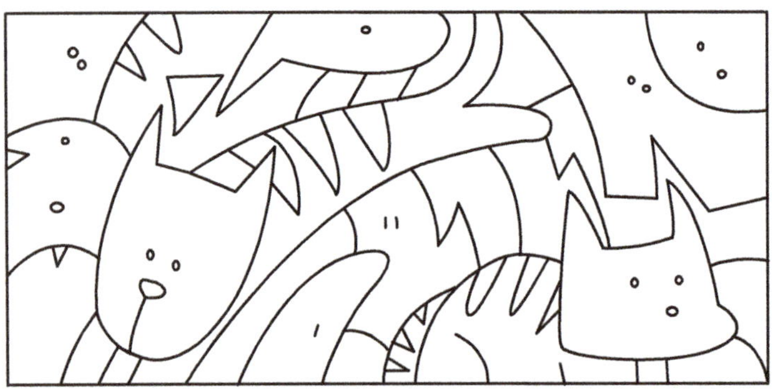

__________ __________ __________.

_______________ _______________.

4. They're oranges.

__________ __________ __________.

_______________ _______________.

Are they...?

Are they cats? Yes, they are.

No, they aren't. They're teachers!

1 Look, write, and match.

1. Are they lunch boxes?
2. Are they pens?
3. ______ ______ rulers?
4. ______ ______ pictures?
5. ______ ______ pencils?
6. ______ ______ books?

Yes, they're books.

No, they aren't. They're pens.

Yes, they're lunch boxes.

No, they aren't. They're pencils.

No, they aren't. They're erasers.

Yes, they're rulers.

1 Listen and write. 2

MRS. SMITH: _Hello_, Lucy!

LUCY PARKS: ______, Mrs. Smith!

Here ______ ______.

______ an apple.

MRS. SMITH: ______ ______!

LUCY PARKS: Good-bye!

MRS. SMITH: __________!

2 Read the dialogue with a friend.

3 Talk with a friend. Then write.

A: Hello, ______!

B: Hi, ______! Here you are.

It's a(n) ________.

A: Thank you!

B: Good-bye.

A: Good-bye!

A: Hello, ______!

B: Hi, ______! Here you are.

They're ________.

A: Thanks!

B: Good-bye.

A: Good-bye!

Let's sing!

1 Listen and draw. 3

Hurray! Yippee!

Hurray! A, A, A, hurray

A, A, A, it's a ______, it's a ______.

A, A, A, hurray Hurray!

Yippee! AN, AN, AN, yippee

AN, AN, AN, it's an ______. It's an ______.

AN, AN, AN, yippee Yippee!

It's an A, hurray!

It's an AN, yippee!

Yippee! Yippee! Yippee!

Hurray!

2 Sort and draw answers from exercise 1.

A	AN

Unit 2

black

blue

brown

gray

green

orange

pink

purple

red

yellow

clock

dog

flowers

hat

house

shirts

table

tree

Colors 4

1 Read, look, and match.

black | blue | brown | green | purple | yellow | red | orange

It's / It isn't + color

1 Follow, color, and write.

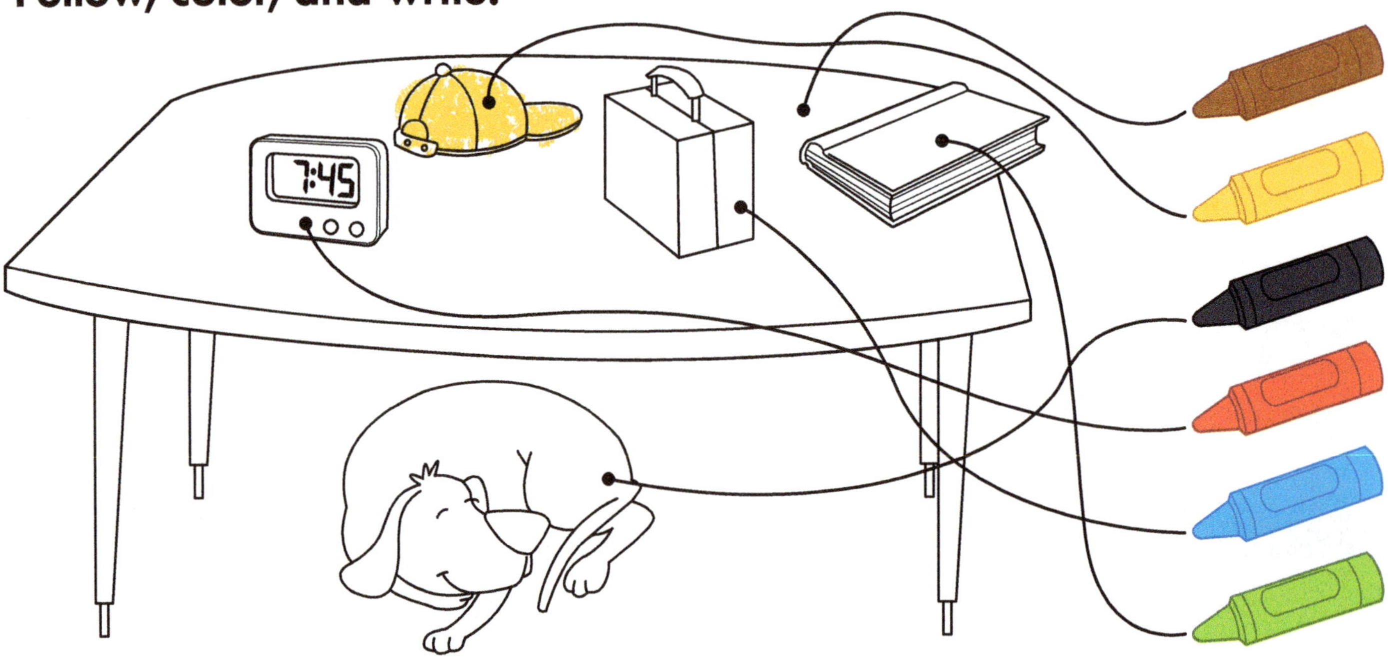

1. The hat __isn't__ red. __It's__ __yellow__.
2. The dog ______ brown. __It's__ ______.
3. The clock ______ yellow. ______ ______.
4. The lunch box ______ pink. ______ ______.
5. The table ______ black. ______ ______.
6. The book ______ blue. ______ ______.

They're / They aren't + color

1 Read, look, and mark (✓).

1

 ✓  ☐

The apples aren't red.
They're green.

2

 ☐  ☐

The hats aren't blue.
They're yellow.

3

 ☐  ☐

The tables aren't brown.
They're black.

4

 ☐  ☐

The trees aren't green.
They're orange.

2 Look and write.

1. The flowers *aren't* gray.
   They're pink and ________.
2. The T-shirts ________ ________.
   ________ ________.

Is it / Are they...? + color

1 Decode, color, and write.

★ red	▲ yellow	○ green	✕ blue	❑ purple	◗ orange

1. _Is_ the table pink? _No_, it _isn't_. It's _blue_.
2. _Are_ the hats green? _Yes_, they _are_.
3. ____ the shirt yellow? ____, it ________. It's ________.
4. ____ the clocks orange? ____, they ________.
5. ____ the house green? ____, it ________. It's ________.
6. ____ the flowers blue? ____, they ________. They're ________.

What color...?

1 Look, follow, and write.

1. What color __is__ __the__ __house__?
2. What color ______ ______ ______?
3. What color ______ ______ ______?
4. What color ______ ______ ______?
5. What color ______ ______ ______?
6. What color ______ ______ ______?

______ ______.

__They're__ ______.

______ ______.

__It's__ __blue__.

______ ______.

______ ______.

What is it? What are they?

1 Listen, complete, and number. 5

1. What *are* *they*? They're *clocks*.
2. What ______ ______? It's *a* ______.
3. What ______ ______? *It's* ______ ______.
4. What ______ ______? ______ ______.
5. ______ ______ ______? ______ ______ ______.
6. ______ ______ ______? ______ ______.

1

2 Read, complete, and draw. Use colors.

dog | green | houses | purple | red | tree

1. What is it? It's a d o g.

   What color is it? It's ___.

2. What are they? They're ___.

   What color are they? They're ___.

3. What is it? It's a ___.

   What color is it? It's ___.

3 Draw, color, and write.

My artwork

1. What is ___ ?

   ___ ___ ___.

2. What color ___ ___?

   ___ ___.

1 Listen and write. 6

FATHER: ______ ______ the shirts?

GRACE: ______!

FATHER: Thanks.

Where ______ ______ ______?

DANNY: ______!

FATHER: Thank you!

GRACE: Uh, oh.

______ ______ ______?

FATHER: Here. Sorry, Rex!

2 Read the dialogue with a friend.

3 Talk with a friend. Then write.

A: Oh no! My bag!

Where are ______ ______?

B: Here!

A: Thanks!

Where's ______ ______?

B: Here!

A: Thank you.

Let's sing!

1 Listen, read, and complete. 7

Red, Yellow, Yellow, and Blue

1. Red, ______, ______, and ______ Point to something ______
   ______ is my favorite color How about you? (Repeat)
2. ______, ______, ______, and ______ Point to something ______
   ______ is my favorite color How about you? (Repeat)
3. ______, ______, ______, and ______ Point to something ______
   ______ is my favorite color How about you? (Repeat)
4. ______ is my favorite color How about you?
   ______ is my favorite color How about you?
   ______ is my favorite color How about you?

Unit 3

tall (adj)

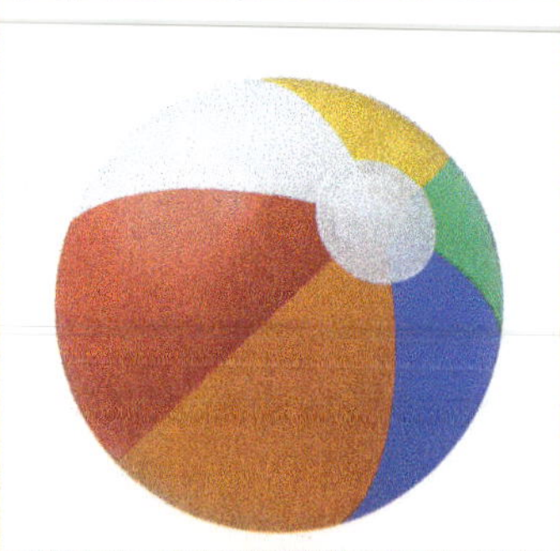

ball

big (adj) small (adj)

short (adj)

bike

car

doll

1 fish, 2 fish

giraffe

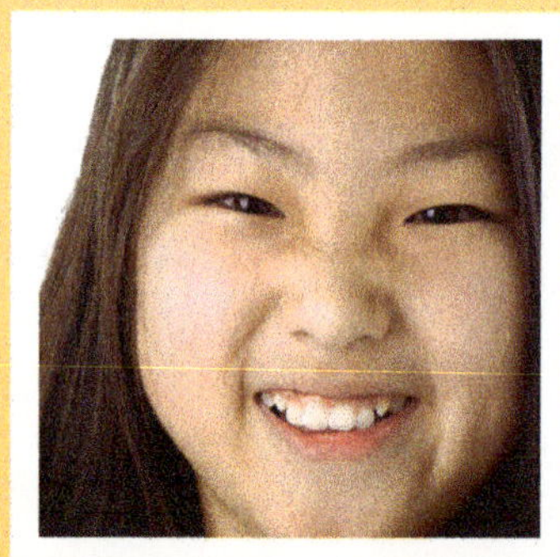

happy (adj)

kite

1 mouse, 2 mice

sad (adj)

teddy bear

truck

Pronouns + *to be*

1 Look and write.

He's
I'm
She's
They're
We're
You're

__I'm__ Jane.

______ Ben.

______ Ann and Amy.

______ Jim.

______ Tina.

______ friends.

2 Look and write.

I'm not Ben.

__I'm Jim.__

You aren't Jane.

______ ______.

We aren't Ben and Amy.

______ ______ ______ ______.

1 Look and write.

1 

DACHSHUND: ___Am___ I tall?

LABRADOR: No, you're not.

___You're___ short.

2 

GIRL 1: ________ he happy?

GIRL 2: Yes, ___he is.___

________ happy.

3 

MOM: ________ they big?

BOY: No, ________ ________.

________ ________.

4 

GIRAFFE 1: ________ we short?

GIRAFFE 2: ________, ________ ________.

________ ________.

This, that

1 Circle and write.

1

This / ***That*** (circled) isn't a kite.

That is a bike.

2

This / ***That*** isn't a mouse.

_____ _____ _____ _____.

3

This / ***That*** isn't a doll.

_____ _____ _____ _____.

4

This / ***That*** isn't a pen.

_____ _____ _____ _____.

5

This / ***That*** isn't a truck.

_____ _____ _____ _____.

6

This / ***That*** isn't a teddy bear.

_____ _____ _____ _____.

Questions with *this, that* 8

1 Look and write.

1 Is this a truck?
No, it isn't.
It's a car.

2 Is this a school?
______, ______ ______.
______ ______ ______.

3 ______ ______ an alien?
______, ______ ______.
______ ______ ______.

4 Is that an elephant?
______, ______ ______.
______ ______ ______.

5 ______ ______ a flower?
______, ______ ______.
______ ______ ______.

This, that with adjectives

This truck is small. Is that truck small? Oh! No, it isn't! It's big!

1 Look and write.

big
happy
red
sad
small
tall

1. ___That___ cat is ______sad______.
2. ___This___ giraffe is ____________.
3. ________ teddy bear is ________.
4. ________ car is ______________.
5. ________ doll is ______________.
6. ________ ball is ______________.

2 Look and write.

1. Is this doll sad? No, she isn't______.
2. Is this ball red?

   __________, __________ __________.
3. Is this bike small?

   __________, __________ __________.

Adjective + noun

1 Read, color, and write.

1. That elephant is big.

It's a *big elephant* ______________.

2. This teacher is happy.

She's a ________ ______________.

3. This hat is short.

It's a ________ ______________.

4. That bike is small.

It's a ________ ______________.

5. That truck is tall.

It's a ________ ______________.

6. This boy is sad.

He's a ________ ______________.

What's this? / What's that?

1 Write, read, and draw.

1. What's ___this___?
2. What's ___that___?
3. What's ________?
4. What's ________?

① 
It's a happy teddy bear.

② It's a blue truck.

③ It's a short giraffe.

④ It's a small teddy bear.

2 Write and draw.

What's this?

It's a ________ ________.

1 Listen and write. 9

ERIC: Hi, Ben! What a *big mouse*!

BEN: This isn't a _______. It's a _______.

ERIC: Oh. _______ a _______ _______!

BEN: _______ that? Is that _______ _______? Is it _______ _______?

ERIC: No, it isn't. This is a _______.

BEN: Wow! _______ a _______ _______!

2 Read the dialogue with a friend.

3 Talk with a friend. Then write.

A: Is that a(n) _______?

B: Yes, _______ _______.

A: What a _______ _______!

B: What's that? Is that a(n) _______?

A: No, it isn't. It's a(n) _______.

B: What a _______ _______!

Let's sing!

1 Listen and complete. Then check (✓). 10

What Is This?

1. What is this?

A bike or a _______?

It is my _______

My blue _______

It is my... favorite toy!

2. What is that?

A boy* or a girl*?

It is my _______

My happy _______

It is my favorite toy!

3. What is that?

Big or _______?

It is our _______

Our blue _______

It is our favorite toy!

boy, girl: see page 44

Unit 4

bag

bed

board

bookcase

glasses

jump (v)

lamp

1 sheep, 2 sheep

shoes

skirt

sleep (v)

socks

sofa

sunglasses

watch

Prepositions *in, on, under*

under the house

in the house

on the house

1 Look and circle.

1 under / in

2 on / in

3 in / on

4 in / on

5 under / on

6 on / under

To be + prepositions, affirmative

The cats **are** **under** the bed.

The mouse **is** **on** the bed.

The mouse **is** **in** the bed!

1 Look and write.

1. The books _____ *are in* _____ the bookcase.
2. The watch ___ *is* ___ _______ the clock.
3. The teddy bear _______ _______ the alien.
4. The lamp _______ _______ the bookcase.
5. The pencil _______ _______ the box.
6. The blue flowers _______ _______ the lamp.
7. The shoes _______ _______ the bookcase.
8. The socks _______ _______ the shoes.

To be + prepositions, negative 11

1 Decode and write.

1  + ~~on~~ +  = *The shoes aren't on the table* ______.

2  + ~~in~~ +  = ______ ______ ______ ______ ______ ______.

3  + ~~under~~ +  = ______ ______ ______ ______ ______ ______.

4  + ~~on~~ +  = ______ ______ ______ ______ ______ ______.

1 Color, look, and write.

1. Is the watch on the board? Yes, it is.
2. Are the books on the desk? No, they aren't.
3. ______ the rulers in the box? ________, ________ ________.
4. ______ the pencil on the desk? ________, ________ ________.
5. ______ the lamp on the bookcase? ________, ________ ________.
6. ______ the glasses under the desk? ________, ________ ________.
7. ______ the teddy bear on the board? ________, ________ ________.
8. ______ the books in the bookcase? ________, ________ ________.

Where...?

1 Match and write.

1. Where is the ball?

2. ________ ________ the shirts?

3. ________ ________ the skirt?

4. ________ ________ the cat?

5. ________ ________ the shoes?

6. ________ ________ the dog?

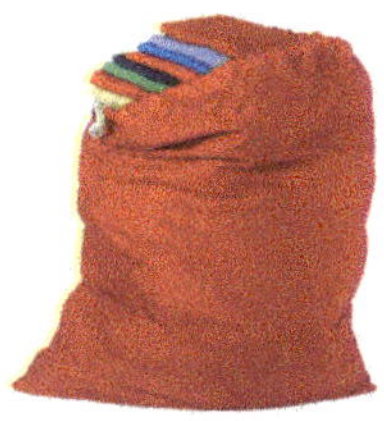

________ ________ the sofa.

They're ________ the bag.

It's under the elephant.

________ ________ the bed.

________ ________ the doll.

________ ________ the box.

2 Listen and color. Listen again and write. 12

1

The *orange* fish *is on* the bookcase.

2

The ________ mouse ______ ______ the box.

3

The ________ shoes ______ ______ the skirts.

4

The ________ hat ______ ______ the giraffe.

5

The ________ dog ______ ______ the bed.

6

The ________ doll ______ ______ the bag.

3 Read, look, and write.

1. *Where are* Nick and May? *They're on the playground*.
2. ______ *is* Tony? *He's* ______ ______ ______.
3. ______ ______ the oranges? ______ ______ ______ ______.
4. ______ ______ the dog? ______ ______ ______ ______.
5. ______ ______ Jill? ______ ______ ______ ______.
6. ______ ______ the apples? ______ ______ ______ ______.

4 Read, write, and draw.

Where ______ you?

I'm ______ ______ ______.

1 Listen and circle. 13

SUE: Let's ***write*** / ***read*** a book.

ANN: No. Let's ***color*** / ***draw*** a picture.

KIM: No. Let's ***jump*** / ***sleep***.

ALL: No, no, no!

SUE: I know! Let's ***sleep*** / ***jump*** on the bed!

2 Read the dialogue with two friends.

3 Talk with two friends. Then write.

A: Let's ____________________.

B: No. Let's ____________________.

C: ______. Let's ____________________!

A: Okay.

B: Cool!

C: Let's go!

Let's sing!

1 Listen. Then color. 14

Where, Oh, Where?

1. Where, oh, where,
   Where is my

2. Where, oh, where?
   Where are my

3. Where, oh, where?
   We can't see them anywhere!
   Where, oh, where?
   We can't see them anywhere!

4. Where, oh, where,
   Where is my

5. Where, oh, where?
   Where are my

6. Where, oh, where?
   We can't see them anywhere!
   Help us! Help us!
   Help us, please!
   We can't see them anywhere!
   Help us, please!

Unit 5

balloon

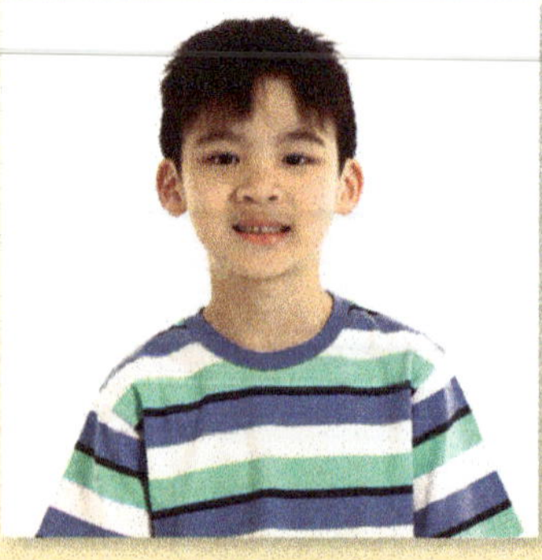
boy

chair

chicken

clown

computer

door

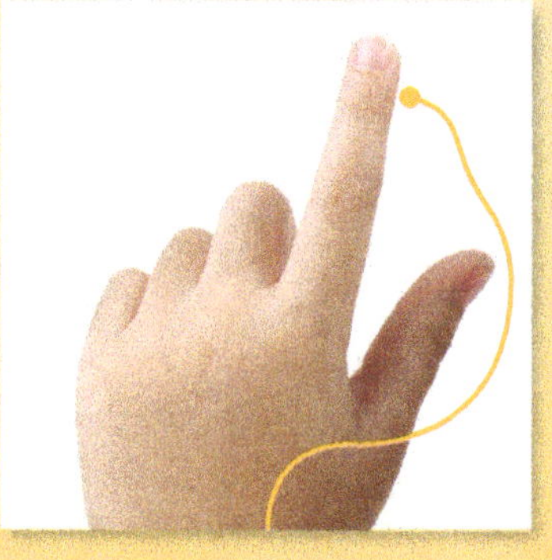
finger

fly (*v*)

girl

name

phone

robot

snake

window

There is / There's 15

There is a ball.

There's a window.

Oh no!
There's a problem!

1 Look and write.

There's a...
There's an...

1. *There's a teacher* ______________________.
2. There's a ______________________.
3. There's ______ ______________________.
4. There's ______ ______________________.
5. ________ ______ ______________.
6. ________ ______ ______________.
7. ________ ______ ______________.
8. ________ ______ ______________.

There are two clowns.

There are two elephants.

No, there are four elephants!

1 Color, count, and write.

book =

chair =

computer =

name =

pencil =

ruler =

1. *There are three* ______ names.
2. There ______ ______ computers.
3. There ______ ______ ______.
4. There ______ ______ ______.
5. ______ ______ ______ ______.
6. ______ ______ ______ ______.

Is there...?

1 Complete and write.

1. *Is there a* ________ book?

   Yes, *there is* ________.

2. *Is there a* ________ boy?

   No, ________ ________.

3. ________ ________ ________ board?

   Yes, ________ ________.

4. ________ ________ ________ phone?

   ________, ________ ________.

5. ________ ________ ________ door?

   ________, ________ ________.

6. ________ ________ ________ teacher?

   ________, ________ ________.

7. ________ ________ ________ book?

   ________, ________ ________.

8. ________ ________ ________ pencil?

   ________, ________ ________.

1 Label and write.

1. *Are there* ________ balls? Yes, *there are* ________.
2. Are ________ bikes? No, ________ ________.
3. ________ ________ kites? ________, ________ ________.
4. ________ ________ cars? ________, ________ ________.
5. ________ ________ balloons? ________, ________ ________.
6. ________ ________ teddy bears? ________, ________ ________.
7. ________ ________ robots? ________, ________ ________.
8. ________ ________ dolls? ________, ________ ________.

How many...?

How many T-shirts are there?

There are eight T-shirts!

1 Color, count, and write.

1. How many watches are there? *There are two watches*____________.
2. *How many* T-shirts are there? ______ ______ ______ ______.
3. ______ ______ skirts are there? ______ ______ ______ ______.
4. ______ ______ shirts are there? ______ ______ ______ ______.
5. ______ ______ socks are there? ______ ______ ______ ______.
6. ______ ______ dresses are there? ______ ______ ______ ______.

2 Read and draw. Use colors.

1

There are four dogs.

2

There are two cats.

3

There are four chickens.

4

There is a fish.

5

There are two giraffes.

6

There are five snakes.

3 Write.

1. What color are the dogs? *They are orange* ________.
2. What color are the cats? They are ________.
3. ______ ______ are the chickens? ______ ______ ______.
4. ______ ______ is the fish? ______ ______ ______.
5. ______ ______ the giraffes? ______ ______ ______.
6. ______ ______ the snakes? ______ ______ ______.

Commands

1 Trace and write.

Fly Listen Open Stand up

1

_____Listen_____!

2

__________ the door!

3

__________!

4

__________ __________!

Let's talk!

1 Listen and write. 16

KIM: Hi, Dan. What's your favorite color?

DAN: It's ___blue___. And yours?

KIM: My favorite color is __________.

BILL: Mine's __________.

2 Read the dialogue with two friends.

3 Talk with a friend. Then write.

A: Hi, __________. What's your favorite animal?

B: It's the __________. And yours?

A: My favorite animal is the __________!

C: Mine's the __________.

Let's sing!

1 Listen, imagine, and draw the ending. 17

There's a Clown

There's a clown
In the classroom.
There are balloons,
There are balloons.
Flying out the
window,
He's flying out the
window.
Look at that clown!
Bye-bye, clown!

Unit 6

ear eye

mouth head nose

arm

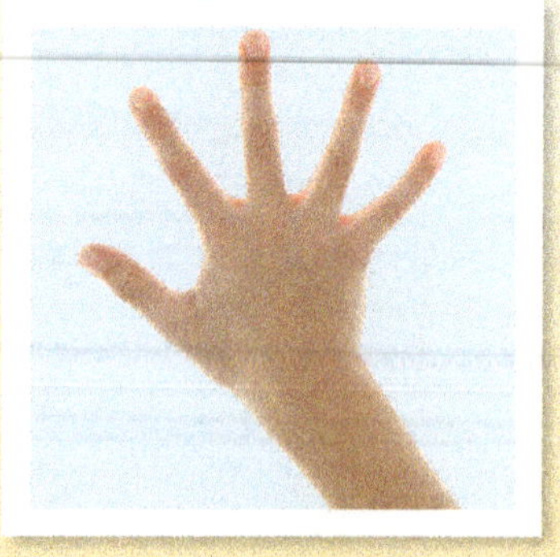

hand

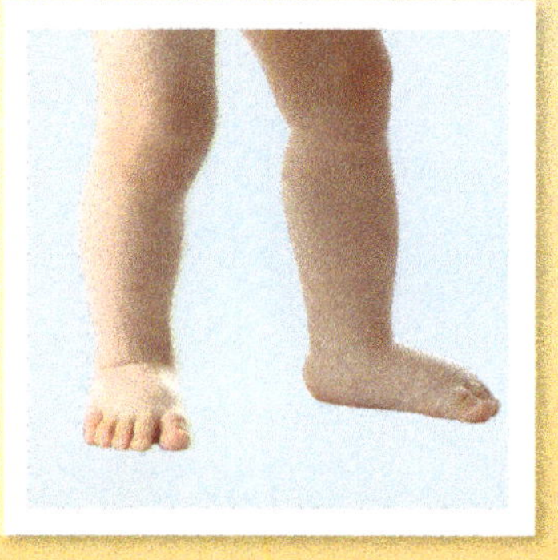

legs

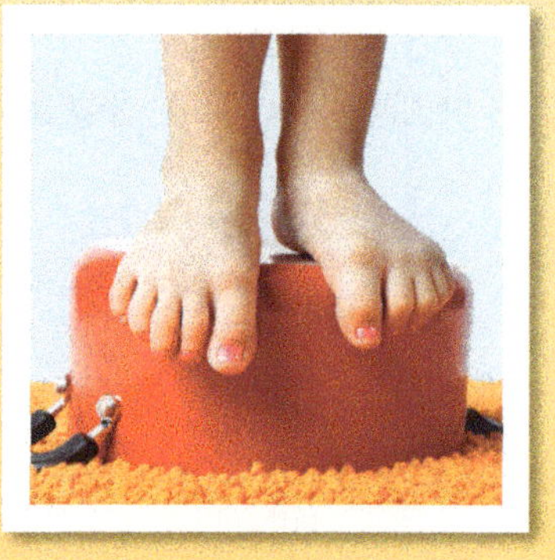

1 foot, 2 feet

play basketball, soccer (v)

play the guitar, the piano (v)

paint (v)

run (v)

sing (v)

swim (v)

Can for ability, affirmative 18

1 Look and solve.

I can

He can

They can

She can

You can

in my arms.

We can

Can for ability, negative

1 Look and write.

color play basketball play the piano read sleep swim

1 

I *can't read* ________ .

2 

She ________ ________.

3 

We ______ ______ ______ ______.

4 

They ________ ________ ________.

5 

You ________ ________!

6 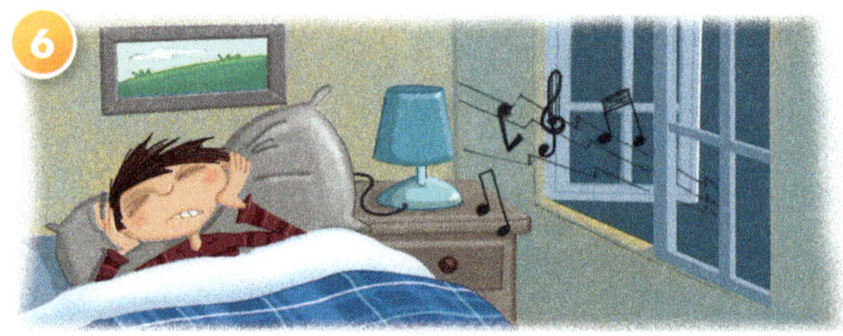

He ________ ________.

Can for ability, interrogative 19

Can the dogs sleep? No, they can't.

Can they sing? Yes, they can!

1 Follow and write.

1. Can she ______ play the guitar? No, she can't ______.
2. ______ they fly? No , they ______.
3. ______ ______ paint? Yes , ______ ______.
4. ______ ______ ______? ______, ______ ______.
5. ______ ______ play soccer? ______, ______ ______.

2 Answer for yourself.

1. Can you read? ______, ______ ______.
2. Can you play the piano? ______, ______ ______.

Possessive adjectives, affirmative

1 Read, circle, and number.

I	you	he	she	it	we	you	they
my	your	his	her	its	our	your	their

1

1. ***I*** / ***My*** can't paint.
   I / ***My*** ears are blue.
2. ***He*** / ***His*** shirt is yellow.
   He / ***His*** can play basketball.
3. ***She*** / ***Her*** mouth is pink.
   She / ***Her*** can sing.
4. ***It*** / ***Its*** head is brown.
   It / ***Its*** can run.
5. ***We*** / ***Our*** can't sing.
   We / ***Our*** feet are orange.
6. ***They*** / ***Their*** eyes are red.
   They / ***Their*** can run.

Possessive adjectives, interrogative

1 Read, match, and write.

1. Are your ears small?
   No, they aren't.
   My ears are big.

2. ______ their arms long?
   Yes, ______ ______.
   Their arms are long.

3. ______ ______ ______ purple?
   No, ______ ______.
   Our noses are red.

4. ______ ______ ______ happy?
   Yes, ______ ______.
   Her doll is happy.

5. ______ ______ ______ pink?
   No, ______ ______.
   His hands are green.

Wh-questions, possessive adjectives

1 Listen and write. 20

1. What's her ______ name?
   Her name is ______ .
2. ______ his ______ name?
   ______ ______ ______ ______.
3. What color is ______ her dress?
   It's ______ yellow ______.
4. ______ ______ are ______ her eyes? They're ______.
5. ______ ______ ______ his shirt? ______ ______.
6. ______ ______ is their piano? ______ ______.

2 Write. Then, draw yourself. Use colors.

1. What's your name?
   ______ ______ ______
   ______.
2. What color are your eyes?
   ______ ______ ______ ______.

3 Read, look, and write.

in
next to
on
under

1

Where are our bikes?

They're under the trees.

2

Where is her hat?

It's ______ her chair.

3

______ ______ ______ sunglasses?

______ ______ the dog.

4

______ ______ ______ guitar?

______ ______ ______ his legs.

5

______ ______ ______ truck?

______ ______ the bag.

6

______ ______ ______ shoes?

______ ______ the chair.

1 Listen and label the boys. 21

NICK: That soccer ball is mine.
Is this basketball yours?

COLIN: Yes, that's mine. Thank you!

NICK: My name is Nick. What's yours?

COLIN: My name is Colin.

NICK: Sorry, I don't understand.
How do you spell that?

COLIN: C-O-L-I-N. Colin.

NICK: Oh! Nice to meet you, Colin.

__________ __________

2 Read the dialogue with a friend.

3 Talk with a friend. Then write.

A: This __________ is mine. Is that __________ yours?

B: Yes. This is mine. It's my favorite __________.

A: My name is __________. What's yours?

B: My name is __________.

A: Sorry. I don't understand.
How do you spell that?

B: __________. __________.

A: Oh. Nice to meet you,
__________!

Let's sing!

1 Listen and order. 22

Let's!

[ ] 

Let's play and fly.

[ ] 

It's day and I'm happy.

[ ] 

Let's jump to the sky.

[1] 

Let's climb a tree.

[ ] 

Let's swim in the sea.

[ ] 

Let's stand up and run.

[ ] 

It's night and I'm sleepy.

[6] 

Let's have some fun.

[ ] 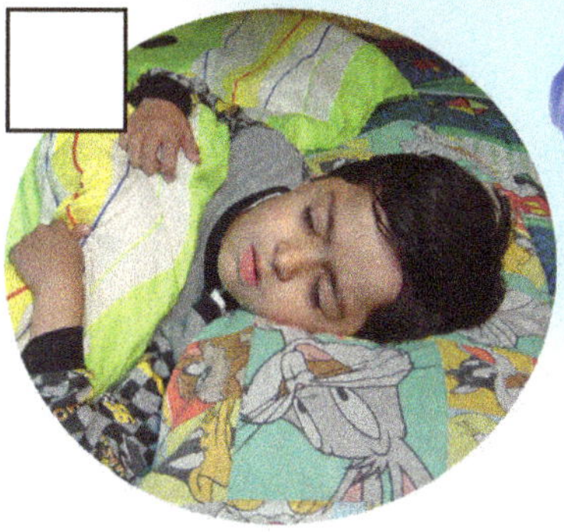

Let's sleep very soon.

[ ] 

Let's look at the moon.

Unit 7

drink

eat

frog (*n*)

smile (*n*, *v*)

ride a bike, a horse

sit

stand

take a picture

talk listen

tiger (*n*)

throw

catch

wear a hat, glasses

How old are you?

1 Find, color, and write.

1

How old is ______ Bill?

He's eight ______.

2

How old am ______ I?

You're ______ ______.

3

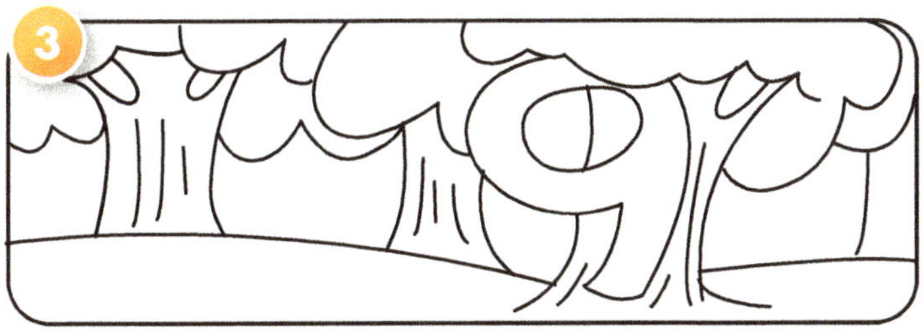

______ ______ are ______ we?

______ ______.

4

______ ______ ______ Jill?

______ ______.

5

______ ______ ______ it?

______ ______.

6

______ ______ ______ they?

______ ______.

Continuous verb forms

sitting

jumping

1 Look and write.

eat   jump   ride a horse   run   sit   swim   take a picture   throw

1. ______ *swimming* ______
2. ______ *eating* ______
3. ____________________
4. ____________________
5. ____________________
6. ____________________
7. ____________________
8. ____________________

Present continuous, affirmative

1 Color and write.

1

You're *swimming* ________.

2

She's *riding a bike* ________.

3

We're ________________.

4

They're ________________.

5

He's ________ ____ ________.

6

I'm ________ ____ ________.

Present continuous, negative 23

He **isn't playing basketball**!

1 Circle, look, and unscramble.

1

They ***isn't*** / ***aren't*** ~~circled: aren't~~ smiling.

2

She ***isn't*** / ***aren't*** ___________.

3

He ***isn't*** / ***aren't*** ___________.

4

We ***isn't*** / ***aren't*** ___________.

5

You ***isn't*** / ***aren't*** ___________.

6

It ***isn't*** / ***aren't*** ___________.

Present continuous, interrogative

1 Look, decode, and write.

1. you + read +  = 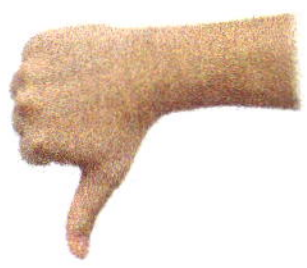

   Are you reading a book? ____ ?   No, I'm not ____ .

2. she + eat +  = 

   Is ____ ____ an ____ ?   Yes, ____ ____ .

3. Sam + draw +  = 

   ____ Sam ____ ____ ____ ?   ____, ____ ____ .

4. we + throw +  = 

   ____ ____ ____ ____ ____ ?   ____, ____ ____ .

5. you + wear +  = 

   ____ ____ ____ ____ ?   ____, ____ ____ .

6. they + ride +  = 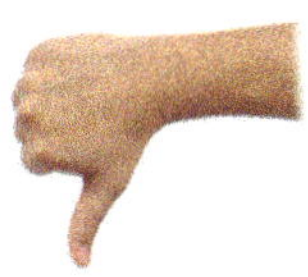

   ____ ____ ____ ____ ?   ____, ____ ____ .

Present continuous, *How many...?*

1 Read, count, and write.

1. *How many* girls *are* standing? *Three girls are standing*.
2. ______ ______ girls ______ singing? *One girl is singing*.
3. ______ ______ boys ______ running? ______ ______ ______ ______.
4. ______ ______ boys ______ drinking? ______ ______ ______ ______.
5. ______ ______ frogs ______ jumping? ______ ______ ______ ______.
6. ______ ______ boys ______ wearing glasses? ______ ______ ______ ______ ______.

2 Choose, circle, and write.

1

Dan is playing the guitar on the sofa.

2

Kim is sitting ______ ______ ______.

3

Sue is ________ ______ ______ ______.

4

Nick is ________ ______ ______ ______.

3 Write, circle, and draw.

I'm ____________ ***in / on / under*** ________ ________.

1 Listen and write. 24

GRACE BELL: Look. Who *is running*_____?

MRS. BELL: Sam _____ __________.

ANNA BELL: Which boy _____ __________?

MRS. BELL: That's Tony.

GRACE BELL: Who _____ __________ the ball? She's __________ a red shirt.

MRS. BELL: That's me!

2 Read the dialogue with two friends.

3 Talk with a friend. Then write.

A: Who is ____________________? B: __________.

A: Which girl / boy is __________? B: __________.

Let's sing!

1 Sing along. 25

Is Grandma Singing?

Is Grandma singing? No, she isn't.
Is Grandma cooking? No, she isn't.
What is she doing? She's watching TV.
Writing, reading, cutting, or cooking,
Writing, reading, cutting, or cooking,
Everybody's doing something right now,
Everybody's doing something right now, hey!
Is Grandpa reading? No, he isn't.
Is Grandpa writing? No, he isn't.
What is he doing? He's cutting a tree.
Writing, reading, cutting or cooking,
Writing, reading, cutting or cooking,
Everybody's doing something right now.
Everybody's doing something right now, hey!

Unit 8

grandfather, grandpa

grandmother, grandma

mother, mom

father, dad

sister

brother

banana

bread

carrot

grapes

ice cream

milk

pear

sausage

tomato

water

Like, affirmative

1 Write and match.

like likes

1. He ___likes___ tomatoes.

2. She __________ bananas.

3. We __________ sausages.

4. It __________ milk.

5. I __________ bread.

6. They __________ grapes.

1 Follow and write.

1 Sue | 2 I | 3 You | 4 Tony | 5 We | 6 She

don't like | doesn't like

1. Sue doesn't like frogs ______________.
2. I ______ don't ______ ______________ ______________.
3. ______ ______ ______________ ______________.
4. ______ ______ ______________ ______________.
5. ______ ______ ______________ ______________.
6. ______ ______ ______________ ______________.

2 Look and circle.

Grandpa	✗	✓	✓	✓
Grandma	✓	✓	✗	✓
Dad	✓	✗	✓	✓
Mom	✗	✓	✗	✓
Anna	✓	✗	✗	✓
Nick	✓	✓	✓	✗

1. My grandfather ***likes*** / ***doesn't like*** tomatoes.
2. My grandmother ***likes*** / ***doesn't like*** sausages.
3. My father and mother ***like*** / ***don't like*** bread.
4. My sister ***likes*** / ***doesn't like*** tomatoes.
5. My brother ***likes*** / ***doesn't like*** carrots.

3 Draw, mark (✓ or ✗), and write.

My name: ________				

1. I ________________ carrots.
2. I ________________ tomatoes.
3. ________________________.
4. ________________________.

1 Look and write.

1. JANE: I *have water* ______.
2. MARY: The dog ___*has*___ a ______.
3. PETER: My brother Jim ______ a ______.
4. SALLY: Paul and Jack ______ ______.
5. DAISY & LILY: We ______ ______.
6. NICK: You ______ a ______.

Have, negative

1 Write and circle.

doesn't have   don't have

1 

She *doesn't have* grapes.

2 

They ______ ______ a dog.

3 

We ______ ______ water.

4 

I ______ ______ ice cream!

5 

You ______ ______ sunglasses.

6 

She ______ ______ a sister.

2 Look, read, and write.

big blue little orange

1

BILLY: I have ___little___ shoes.

You have ___big___ shoes.

CLOWN: I have a ____________ nose.

You have a ____________ nose.

2

CLOWN: Look. We have balloons!

I have a ____________ balloon, and

you have an ____________ balloon.

BILLY: Yes, but I don't like ____________ balloons.

3

CLOWN: That's okay. Now you have

a ____________ balloon!

BILLY: Thank you! I like ____________

balloons!

3 Look and circle.

1. The clown *has* / *doesn't have* a black hat.
2. Billy *has* / *doesn't have* a red nose.
3. The teddy bear *has* / *doesn't have* a pink shirt.
4. They *have* / *don't have* happy faces.

4 Listen and write. 27

1

 → 3 

Jill *has three chickens*.

2

 → ____ 

I ________ ________ ________.

3

 → ____ 

She ________ ________ ________.

4

 → ____ 

We ________ ________ ________.

5

 → ____ 

My grandmother ________ ________ ________.

6

 → ____ 

My brothers ________ ________ ________.

5 Write and draw.

1. I have ____________________.
2. I like ____________________.

1 Listen and write. 28

BEN: Look! She has a *yellow pear*.

JILL: I have a ________ ________, too.

ANN: I don't have a ________ ________.

I have ________ ________.

JILL: I like ________ ________.

BEN: I like ________ ________, too!

ANN: Here, some ________.

BEN AND JILL: Thank you!

2 Read the dialogue with two friends.

3 Talk with two friends. Then write.

A: Look. He / She has ________________.

B: I have ________________, too.

C: I don't have ________________.

I have ________________.

B: I like ________________.

A: I like ________________, too.

Let's sing!

1 Listen, match, and write. 29

We Like Food

1. Do you like pizza? — Yes, I do. My grandma and my grandpa like _____ _____, too.

2. Do you like oranges? — Yes, I do. My aunt and my uncle like __________, too.

3. Do you like ice cream? — Yes, I do. My cousin and my brothers like __________, too.

2 Write and sing.

Do you like __________?
Yes, I do. My __________
and my __________
like __________, too.

Grammar summary

Units 1, 2, and 3

To be, affirmative			
I	am	(I'm)	Ann.
You	are	(You're)	happy.
He She It	is	(He's) (She's) (It's)	on the table.
We You They	are	(We're) (You're) (They're)	brothers.

To be, negative				
I	am	not	(I'm not)	Jill.
You	are		(You aren't)	a student.
He She It	is		(He isn't) (She isn't) (It isn't)	in the house.
We You They	are		(We aren't) (You aren't) (They aren't)	tall.

Be, interrogative			
Am	I	short?	Yes, you are. / No, you're not.
Are	you	under the bed?	Yes, I am. / No, I'm not.
Is	he she it	black and white?	Yes, he is. / No, he isn't. Yes, she is. / No, she isn't. Yes, it is. / No, it isn't.
Are	we you they	teachers?	Yes, you are. / No, you aren't. Yes, we are. / No, we aren't. Yes, they are. / No, they aren't.

Unit 1

A, an
a book, a desk...
an apple, an elephant...

Unit 2

What color...?			
What color	is	the T-shirt?	It's white.
	are	the cars?	They're orange.

What...?			
What	is	it?	It's a hat.
	are	they?	They're tigers.

What is it? What are they?			
What	is	it?	It's an apple.
	are	they?	They're giraffes.

Unit 3

This, that with nouns

This is a dog. This isn't a cat. Is this a cat? Yes, it is. / No, it isn't. What's this? It's a dog.	That is a cat. That isn't a dog. Is that a dog? Yes, it is. / No, it isn't. What's that? It's a cat.

This, that with adjectives

This truck is big. This truck isn't small. Is this truck big? Yes, it is. / No, it isn't.	That truck is small. That truck isn't big. Is that truck small? Yes, it is. / No, it isn't.

Adjective + noun

The fish is big.	That fish is big.	It's a big fish.

Prepositions *in, on, under*

	in the bag
	on the bag
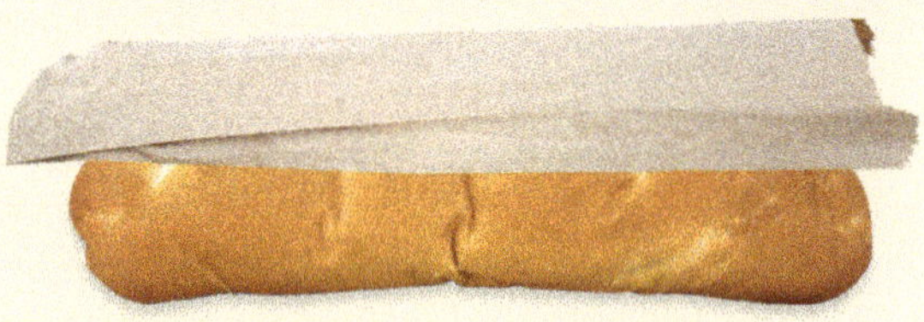	under the bag

Where is it? Where are they?

Where	is	it?	It's under the tree.
	are	they?	They're on the desk.

Unit 4

Unit 5

There is, there are

There is a giraffe. Is there a giraffe? Yes, there is. / No, there isn't.	There are three pencils. Are there three pencils? Yes, there are. / No, there aren't.

How many...?

How many watches are there?	There are five watches. There is one watch.

Commands

Look! Write! Listen! Talk!

Unit 6

Can for ability, affirmative

I	can	run.
You		play the piano.
He She It		jump.
We You They		read.

Can for ability, negative

I	can't	swim.
You		play the guitar.
He She It		sing.
We You They		paint a picture.

Can for ability, interrogative

Can	I	fly?	Yes, you can. / No, you can't.
	you	throw a ball?	Yes, I can. / No, I can't.
	he she it	smile?	Yes, he can. / No, he can't. Yes, she can. / No, she can't. Yes, it can. / No, it can't.
	we you they	play the trumpet?	Yes, you can. / No, you can't. Yes, we can. / No, we can't. Yes, they can. / No, they can't.

Possessive adjectives

This is **my** sock.
That is **your** shoe.
This is **his** book.
That is **her** apple.
This is **its** water.

This is **our** playground.
This is **your** letter.
That is **their** dog.

What's your name?

What's your name? My name is Bill.

Unit 7

Present continuous, affirmative

I	am	(I'm)	talking. listening. jumping rope. riding a horse.
You	are	(You're)	
He She It	is	(He's) (She's) (It's)	
We You They	are	(We're) (You're) (They're)	

How old are you?

How old are you?
I'm seven.

Present continuous, negative				
I	am		(I'm not)	
You	are		(You aren't)	
He She It	is	not	(He isn't) (She isn't) (It isn't)	sitting. eating. riding a bike. taking a picture.
We You They	are		(We aren't) (You aren't) (They aren't)	

Present continuous, interrogative			
Am	I		Yes, you are. / No, you're not.
Are	you		Yes, I am. / No, I'm not.
Is	he she it	smiling? running? throwing a ball? wearing a hat?	Yes, he is. / No, he isn't. Yes, she is. / No, she isn't. Yes, it is. / No, it isn't.
Are	we you they		Yes, you are. / No, you aren't. Yes, we are. / No, we aren't. Yes, they are. / No, they aren't.

***Like*, affirmative**		
I You	like	pears.
He She It	likes	bread.
We You They	like	small tomatoes.

***Like*, negative**			
I You	don't	like	milk.
He She It	doesn't	like	big hats.
We You They	don't	like	frogs.

***Have*, affirmative**		
I You	have	two eyes.
He She It	has	a pear.
We You They	have	yellow bananas.

***Have*, negative**			
I You	don't	have	a big dog.
He She It	doesn't		a purple pen.
We You They	don't		grapes.

Audio script

Unit 1

Track 1
TEACHER: Look.
GIRL: A school?
BOY: An elephant?
TEACHER: No. A playground!
CHILDREN: Hooray!

Track 2
MRS. SMITH: Hello, Lucy!
LUCY PARKS: Hello, Mrs. Smith! Here you are. It's an apple.
MRS. SMITH: Thank you!
LUCY PARKS: Good-bye!
MRS. SMITH: Good-bye!

Track 3
Hurray! Yippee!
Hurray!
A, A, A, hurray
A, A, A, it's a book, it's a pen.
A, A, A, hurray! Hurray!

Yippee!
AN, AN, AN, yippee
AN, AN, AN, it's an apple. It's an eraser.
AN, AN, AN, yippee
Yippee!

It's an A, hurray!
It's an AN, yippee!
Yippee! Yippee! Yippee!
Hurray!

Unit 2

Track 4
CROWD 1: Go, Red!
CROWD 2: Go, Blue!
CROWD 1: Red!
CROWD 2: Blue!
CROWD 1: Red!
CROWD 2: Blue!
CROWD 2: Blue! Blue!
ANNOUNCER: Gooooooal!

Track 5
1. What are they? (sounds of clocks ticking)
2. What is it? (sound of a pencil scratching on paper)
3. What is it? (playground sounds)
4. What are they? (sounds of dogs barking)
5. What is it? (sound of an elephant trumpeting)
6. What are they? (sounds of cats meowing)

Track 6
FATHER: Where are the shirts?
GRACE: Here!
FATHER: Thanks. Where are the hats?
DANNY: Here!
FATHER: Thank you!
GRACE: Uh, oh. Where's the dog?
FATHER: Here. Sorry, Rex!

Track 7
Red, Yellow, Yellow, and Blue
Red, yellow, yellow, and blue
Point to something yellow
Yellow is my favorite color
How about you? (Repeat)

Red, red, yellow and blue
Point to something red
Red is my favorite color
How about you? (Repeat)

Red, yellow, blue, and blue
Point to something blue
Blue is my favorite color
How about you? (Repeat)

Blue is my favorite color
How about you?
Yellow is my favorite color
How about you?
Red is my favorite color
How about you? (3x)

Unit 3

Track 8
MAY: Hey, Alice, is this a hat?
ALICE: No, it isn't. It's a cat!
MAY: Oh!

Track 9
ERIC: Hi, Ben! What a big mouse!
BEN: This isn't a mouse. It's a dog.
ERIC: Oh. What a small dog!
BEN: What's that? Is that a giraffe? Is it an elephant?
ERIC: No, it isn't. This is a dog.
BEN: Wow! What a tall dog!

Track 10
What Is This?

What is this?
A bike or a car?
It is my truck
My blue truck
It is my… favorite toy!

What is that?
A boy or a girl?
It is my doll
My happy doll
It is my favorite toy!

What is that?
Big or small?
It is our kite
Our blue kite
It is our favorite toy!

Unit 4

Track 11
DAD: Whoa-OAH!
BOY: Hi, Dad. Oh! The books aren't in the bookcase!
DAD: No, they aren't. And look. The car isn't in the box!
BOY: Oops!

Track 12
1. Where is the orange fish?
   The orange fish is ON the bookcase.
2. Where is the gray mouse?
   The gray mouse is IN the box.
3. Where are the red shoes?
   The red shoes are UNDER the skirts.
4. Where is the blue hat?
   The blue hat is ON the giraffe.
5. Where is the brown dog?
   The brown dog is UNDER the bed.
6. Where is the pink doll?
   The pink doll is IN the bag.

Track 13
SUE: Let's read a book.
ANN: No. Let's color a picture.
KIM: No. Let's sleep.
ALL: No, no, no!
SUE: I know! Let's jump on the bed!
ALL: Cool! Okay! Yay!

Track 14
Where, Oh, Where?

Where, oh, where,
Where is my ball?
Where, oh, where,
Where are my dolls?

Where, oh, where?
We can't see them anywhere!

Where, oh, where,
Where is my teddy bear?
Where oh, where,
Where are my cars?

Where, oh, where?
We can't see them anywhere!

Help us! Help us! Help us, please!
We can't see them anywhere!
Help us, please!

Unit 5

Track 15

There is a ball.
There's a window.
Oh no! There's a problem!

Track 16

KIM: Hi, Dan. What's your favorite color?
DAN: It's blue. And yours?
KIM: My favorite color is yellow.
BILL: Mine's orange!

Track 17

There's a Clown

There's a clown
In the classroom.
There are balloons,
There are balloons.
Flying out the window,
(He's) flying out the window.
Look at that clown!
Bye-bye, clown! (Repeat)

Unit 6

Track 18

CHILD 1: I can run!
CHILD 2: You can jump!
CHILD 3: We can sing!
WOMAN: Stop!
ALL CHILDREN: Sorry, Mom!

Track 19

GIRL: Can the dogs sleep?
BOY: No, they can't. It's a full moon!
GIRL: Can they sing?
BOY: Yes, they can. Listen!

Track 20

JILL: My name is Jill.
DAN: My name is Dan.
JILL: My dress is pink.
My eyes are green.
DAN: My shirt is yellow.
JILL and DAN: Our piano is blue. Let's play! 1, 2, 3...

Track 21

NICK and COLIN: Wait! / Stop! / Oops! / Oh no!
NICK: That soccer ball is mine. Is this basketball yours?
COLIN: Yes, that's mine. Thank you!
NICK: My name is Nick. What's yours?
COLIN: My name is Colin.
NICK: Sorry. I don't understand. How do you spell that?
COLIN: C-O-L-I-N. Colin.
NICK: Oh! Nice to meet you, Colin.

Track 22

Let's!

Let's climb a tree.
Let's swim in the sea.
Let's play and fly.
Let's jump to the sky.
It's day, and I'm happy.

Let's have some fun.
Let's stand up and run.
Let's look at the moon.
Let's sleep very soon.
It's night, and I'm sleepy.

It's day, and I'm happy.
It's night, and I'm sleepy.

Unit 7

Track 23

GIRL: They're playing basketball. Oh! Look!
COACH: Wait a minute! He isn't playing basketball! He's riding a bike!

Track 24

GRACE BELL: Look. Who is running?
MRS. BELL: Sam is running.
ANNA BELL: Which boy is smiling?
MRS. BELL: That's Tony.
GRACE BELL: Who is catching the ball? She's wearing a red shirt.
MRS. BELL: That's me!

Track 25

Is Grandma Singing?

Is Grandma singing?
No, she isn't.
Is Grandma cooking?
No, she isn't.
What is she doing?
She's watching TV.

(Chorus:)
Writing, reading, cutting, or cooking,
Writing, reading, cutting, or cooking,
Everybody's doing something right now,
Everybody's doing something right now, hey!

Is Grandpa reading?
No, he isn't.
Is Grandpa writing?
No, he isn't.
What is he doing?
He's cutting a tree.

(Chorus)

Unit 8

Track 26

GIRL: My sister has a dog. My brothers have a dog.
My grandmother has a dog.
But I… I have a fish!

Track 27

BOY 1: Jill has three chickens. Three chickens.
I have one snake. One snake.
BOY 2: My sister has five watches! Five watches.
We have eight clocks. Eight clocks!
GIRL: My grandmother has two cats. Two cats.
My brothers have four robots. Four robots.

Track 28

BEN: She has a yellow pear.
JILL: I have a yellow pear, too.
ANN: I don't have a yellow pear. I have green grapes.
JILL: I like green grapes.
BEN: I like green grapes, too.
ANN: Here, some grapes.
BEN and JILL: Thank you!

Track 29

We Like Food

Do you like pizza?
Yes, I do. My aunt and my uncle like pizza, too.

Do you like oranges?
Yes, I do. My cousin and my brothers like oranges, too.

Do you like ice cream?
Yes, I do. My grandma and my grandpa like
ice cream, too.

Vocabulary